DOG BREEDS

Yorkshire Terriers

by Sara Green

Consultant:
Michael Leuthner, D.V.M.
PetCare Clinic, Madison, Wisc.

BLASTOFF! READERS 4

BELLWETHER MEDIA • MINNEAPOLIS, MN

Note to Librarians, Teachers, and Parents:

Blastoff! Readers are carefully developed by literacy experts and combine standards-based content with developmentally appropriate text.

Level 1 provides the most support through repetition of high-frequency words, light text, predictable sentence patterns, and strong visual support.

Level 2 offers early readers a bit more challenge through varied simple sentences, increased text load, and less repetition of high-frequency words.

Level 3 advances early-fluent readers toward fluency through increased text and concept load, less reliance on visuals, longer sentences, and more literary language.

Level 4 builds reading stamina by providing more text per page, increased use of punctuation, greater variation in sentence patterns, and increasingly challenging vocabulary.

Level 5 encourages children to move from "learning to read" to "reading to learn" by providing even more text, varied writing styles, and less familiar topics.

Whichever book is right for your reader, Blastoff! Readers are the perfect books to build confidence and encourage a love of reading that will last a lifetime!

This edition first published in 2009 by Bellwether Media.

No part of this publication may be reproduced in whole or in part without written permission of the publisher. For information regarding permission, write to Bellwether Media Inc., Attention: Permissions Department, Post Office Box 19349, Minneapolis, MN 55419-0349.

Library of Congress Cataloging-in-Publication Data
Yorkshire terriers / by Sara Green.
    p. cm. — (Blastoff! readers. Dog breeds)
  Includes bibliographical references and index.
  Summary: "Simple text and full color photographs introduce beginning readers to the characteristics of Yorkshire Terriers. Developed by literacy experts for students in kindergarten through third grade"–Provided by publisher.
    ISBN-13: 978-1-60014-214-7 (hardcover : alk. paper)
    ISBN-10: 1-60014-214-1 (hardcover : alk. paper)
  1. Yorkshire terrier—Juvenile literature. I. Title.

SF429.Y6G74 2008
636.76–dc22   2008020005

Contents

What Are Yorkshire Terriers?

The Yorkshire Terrier is a small **breed** of dog. They are often called Yorkies.

Adult Yorkshire Terriers are 6 to 7 inches (15.2 to 17.8 centimeters) tall at the shoulder. They weigh about 7 pounds (3.2 kilograms). Dog breeds that weigh less than 10 pounds (4.5 kilograms) are called **toy breeds**.

Yorkshire Terriers have long, silky, gold and gray **coats**. These coats need care. Dogs with long hair can get **mats**. Yorkshire Terriers need daily **grooming** to keep their long hair free from mats.

Some owners do not want to brush their Yorkshire Terrier's long hair every day. They choose to give their Yorkies haircuts instead. Many of the dogs wear a **topknot** so their hair does not cover their eyes.

fun fact

Yorkshire Terrier puppies are born with black and tan coats. The black color changes to gray as the puppy grows up.

Yorkshire Terriers are born with long tails. Some people take their Yorkshire Terriers to a **veterinarian** to have their tails **docked**. Docking is an operation that removes part of the tail. However, many people choose to keep their Yorkshire Terrier's tail long.

fun fact

The smallest dog in recorded history was a Yorkshire Terrier named Sylvia. She was 2.5 inches (6.4 centimeters) tall and weighed 4 ounces (113.4 grams).

History of Yorkshire Terriers

Yorkshire Terriers come from a mixture of two other types of terriers. More than 100 years ago, many Scottish people moved to England to find work. They brought along their Scottish Terriers.

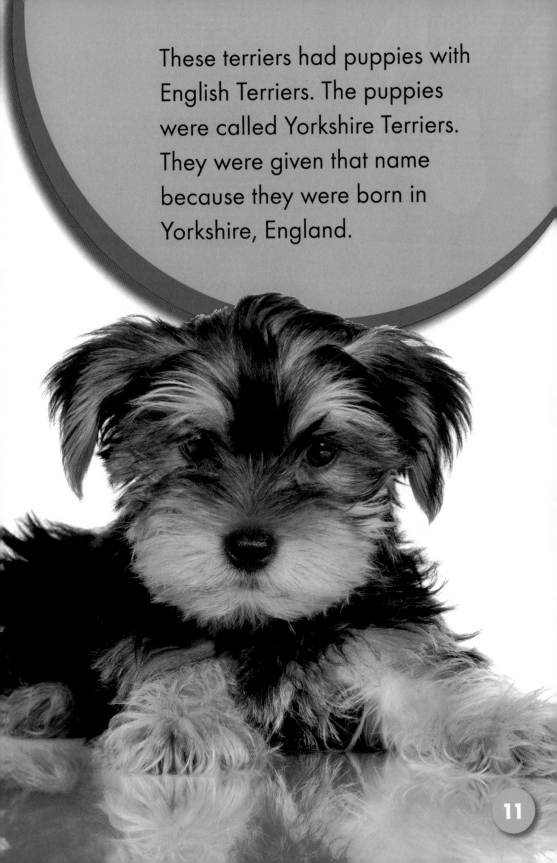

These terriers had puppies with English Terriers. The puppies were called Yorkshire Terriers. They were given that name because they were born in Yorkshire, England.

Not all of the early Yorkshire Terriers were small in size. Some weighed as much as 30 pounds (13.6 kilograms).

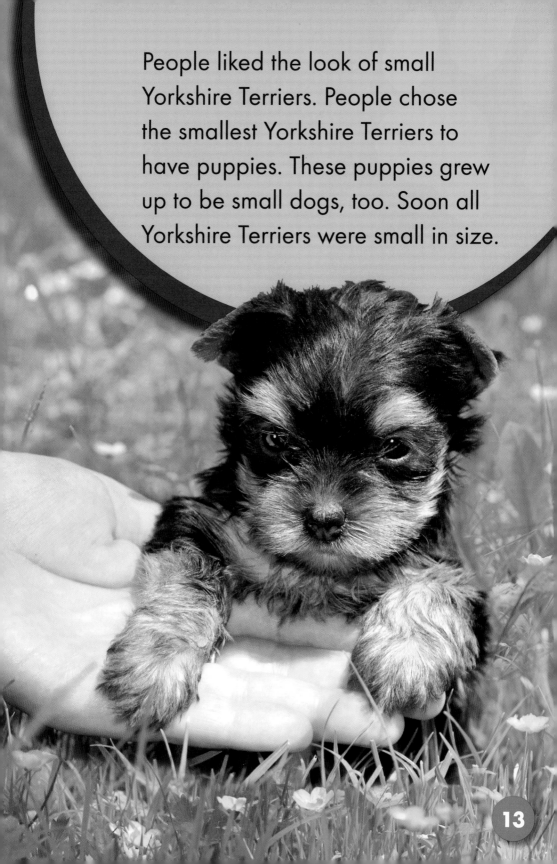

People liked the look of small Yorkshire Terriers. People chose the smallest Yorkshire Terriers to have puppies. These puppies grew up to be small dogs, too. Soon all Yorkshire Terriers were small in size.

At first, people in England kept
Yorkshire Terriers to kill **rodents**.
Then people began to keep them
as house pets.

People brought Yorkshire Terriers to the United States for the first time in 1872. Over time, it became fashionable for American women to carry their Yorkshire Terriers around in their arms or in their purses.

! **fun fact**
Toy breeds were once considered luxury dogs and only owned by royalty.

Yorkshire Terriers Today

Even though they are small, Yorkshire Terriers are very brave dogs. They will bark at strangers. Yorkshire Terriers make a lot of noise for their small size. They are also not afraid to chase rodents just like their **ancestors**.

Some Yorkshire Terriers are used in hospitals
or nursing homes. They visit people who
are sick. The small size of Yorkshire Terriers
means they can easily fit on the beds or laps
of the people they are visiting. Playing with a
Yorkshire Terrier can make people feel happy.

Yorkshire Terriers are quick and intelligent. They do well in the sport of **agility** because they can understand and obey commands from their owners. An agility course has tunnels, ramps, and other objects. Yorkies try to go through the course as fast as they can.

Most Yorkshire Terriers are kept as pets. They are well-suited for this role. They are small dogs with lots of energy and affection to share.

Glossary

agility—a dog sport where dogs run through a series of obstacles

ancestor—a family member who lived long ago

breed—a type of dog

coat—the hair or fur of an animal

docked—shortened by an operation

grooming—taking care of the coat of an animal

mats—snarls in hair that are difficult to comb out

rodents—small mammals that gnaw or nibble such as mice and rats

topknot—a knot of hair at the top of the head tied with a bow or ribbon

toy breeds—breeds that weigh less than 10 pounds (6.1 kilograms) as adults

veterinarian—a doctor who takes care of animals

To Learn More

AT THE LIBRARY

American Kennel Club. *The Complete Dog Book for Kids*. New York: Howell Books, 1996.

Gray, Susan Heinrichs. *Yorkshire Terriers*. Chanhassen, Minn.: Child's World, 2007.

Linden, Joanne. *Yorkshire Terriers*. Mankato, Minn.: Pebble Books, 2006.

ON THE WEB

Learning more about Yorkshire Terriers is as easy as 1, 2, 3.

1. Go to www.factsurfer.com

2. Enter "Yorkshire Terriers" into search box.

3. Click the "Surf" button and you will see a list of related web sites.

With factsurfer.com, finding more information is just a click away.

Index

The images in this book are reproduced through the courtesy of: Joanna Pecha, front cover; Mark Raycroft / Getty Images, pp. 4, 6; Steve Shepard, p. 5; JUNIORS BILDARCHIV / agefotostock, p. 7; Michal Napartowicz, p. 9; Eric Isselée, p. 10 (left), 11; Andreas Gradin, p. 10 (right); Julie Toy / Getty Images, p. 12; Ela Wlodarczyk / Alamy, p. 13; J. LL. Banús / age fotostock, p. 14; eightfish / Getty Images, p. 15; Rolf Hicker / age fotostock, pp. 16-17; Janine Wiedel Photolibrary / Alamy, p. 18; Rebecca Emery / Getty Images, p. 19; Pix 'n Pages, p. 20; Carlos Arranz, p. 21.